CW01512639

Original title:

Bananas in the Breeze

Copyright © 2025 Creative Arts Management OÜ

Author: Levi Montgomery

ISBN HARDBACK: 978-1-80586-359-5
ISBN PAPERBACK: 978-1-80586-831-6

Breezes Full of Life

Wobbling on the tree, what a sight,
Dancing leaves take off, oh, such delight.
A playful gust swoops in to tease,
Laughter swirls amidst the whispering trees.

Fluttering hats take a whimsical flight,
As squirrels giggle under the moonlight.
Nature plays tricks, a comedy spree,
In a world full of joy, can't you see?

Juggling Sunbeams

Sunlight winks, casting shadows so neat,
Juggling moonbeams, oh, what a feat!
Playful chirps from creatures nearby,
They tiptoe on air, oh my, oh my!

A radiant whispers fills the air bright,
Bouncing off petals, a dazzling sight.
Nature's laughter rings out with ease,
As the trees sway gently in the breeze.

Nature's Gentle Trickster

Whirls and twirls in a breezy dance,
Nature's fun games draw us into a trance.
With a flick and a spin, the world's on a roll,
A charming spin leaves us all feeling whole.

Chasing after dreams, we run with our glee,
Tripping on laughter like it's meant to be.
The world is a stage, in vibrant display,
Let's sway with the trickster, come join the play!

Sun-Kissed Revelations

Sunshine tickles the leaves with a grin,
A joyous serenade, let the day begin.
Whispers of fun waft through the air,
As mischievous shadows dance without care.

Crisp laughter bursts from flowers in bloom,
Nature's sweet secret dispels all gloom.
Discovering joy, let's celebrate these,
In this merry moment, we find our ease.

Tropical Whispers of Golden Fruit

In the garden where laughter grows,
Curved peels hide secrets nobody knows.
Swinging softly on branches so free,
They giggle and wiggle, oh what a spree!

With a splash of sun and a hint of cheer,
Each fruit is a jest, tickling the sphere.
They play hide and seek with the buzzing bees,
And dance with the whispers of warm tropical breeze.

Sunlit Serenade of Yellow Waves

A burst of yellow like sunlit beams,
They sway on the trees, crafting wild dreams.
Each wink from the foliage rolls with delight,
Bouncing around in the warm, golden light.

Silly friends dangling, what a fun show,
Waving to passerby; "Look at us grow!"
Tickling the air with their fruity allure,
A sunlit laugh that feels oh-so-pure.

Dancing Curves in the Summer Air

With cheeky curves and a sunny grin,
They jiggle and jive as the day begins.
Dressed in their jackets of vibrant hue,
Gossiping softly, "How are you, too?"

In the balmy air, they twist and twirl,
Swinging so wildly, they give it a whirl.
Each movement a giggle, a comic parade,
Bringing us cheer in their tropical charade.

A Melody of Ripe Sweetness

With sweetness dripping like honey on toast,
They croon lullabies, the summertime boast.
Each pluck from the branch brings a hearty cheer,
To all of us savoring summer's last beer.

In orchards of joy, they sing nice and loud,
"Join us for fun! Come on, be proud!"
Spinning in circles, these fruits take their bows,
The laughter continues, in sunshine they rouse.

A Breezy Tangle of Joy

In the garden, laughter sings,
Twisting vines and flapping wings.
A hat flies high, a trail of glee,
As cheeky squirrels climb the tree.

The sun peeks through the leafy shade,
A dance of shadows, unafraid.
With giggles echoing in the air,
Each playful breeze a whispered dare.

Sunlit Dance of the Grove

Beneath the trees, shadows prance,
The critters gather for a chance.
With tiny feet and wiggly tails,
They jig and jive as laughter trails.

A swing set creaks, a songbird squeals,
The bounce of joy, a world that heals.
In sunshine's glow, they leap and sway,
Spreading cheer, come what may.

Fruitful Fables Untold

Whimsical tales from every fruit,
Talkative pears in a funky suit.
Grapes, they giggle, in a tight-knit bunch,
While apples plot a prank for lunch.

Amidst the fun, the oranges cheer,
Spinning wild in a fruity sphere.
Each tale unfolds with zest and flair,
A juicy life, beyond compare.

Limoncello Dreams Under the Sky

With dreams like bubbles in the air,
Twists and turns without a care.
Lemons bounce with laughter bright,
Painting scenes in pure delight.

In twilight's glow, the fun awakes,
With zesty wishes that the heart makes.
Under stars, they swirl and spin,
A playful dance, let laughter in.

The Breeze's Sweet Caress

In the sunlit air, a wiggle and sway,
Fruits dance about in a jolly display.
A jester of yellow, laughter on show,
With every soft gust, they giggle and blow.

Laughter erupts with a playful twist,
Fruits tumble and bounce, you just can't resist.
Swaying and shaking, they frolic with glee,
The breeze joins the fun, as wild as can be.

Spray of Sundrenched Laughter

With a splash of delight and a wink from the sun,
Silly shadows play; oh, this day is so fun!
The light strikes the peel, a shimmer so bright,
Sun-kissed laughter, taking flight in the light.

Each spark from the skin, a giggle released,\nJuicy
mischief bounces, never to cease.
In this zany realm of fruits and of cheer,
Sunshine chuckles softly; it's joy that we hear.

Tropical Lullabies

Gentle whispers float on the warm, breezy air,
Hilarious tales dance without a care.
Mangoes collide with coconuts so round,
While giggling fruits gather, a wacky sound.

In the shade of the leaves, funny dreams take form,
As daylight chuckles, a playful warm storm.
With every sweet bounce, a new laugh takes flight,
In this quirky kingdom, the day feels just right.

Sweetness on a String

Fruits hanging low like stars in a tree,
Swing to the rhythm, so wild and so free.
A melody soft spills from every bright hue,
Tangled together, a curious crew.

Pull on the laughter, let sweetness ensue,
With every sweet sigh, the whimsy renews.
Tied to the joy, they sway and they sing,
In this jolly world, sweetness is king.

Golden Boughs in the Air

Golden boughs sway, dancing light,
A feast of cheer, what a sight!
Sunshine giggles, shadows play,
Nature chuckles throughout the day.

Frolicsome leaves, a vibrant show,
Tiptoe whispers, sweet and low.
Breeze tickles, frothy delight,
Joyful fruits basking in the light.

Silly squirrels race around,
Chasing giggles, lost and found.
They leap and twirl with carefree glee,
In their world, all wild and free.

Twirling Under the Sun

Twisting tendrils in the sun,
Nature's dance, oh what fun!
Round and round, a jolly spree,
Who can tell what's next to be?

Wobbling buds with laughter bright,
Swinging low, they take to flight.
With each gust, they twist and spin,
A merry game where all can win.

Sunbeams play, shadows tease,
Frolicsome laughter floats with ease.
Round the garden, skip along,
Nature's rhythm, a joyful song.

The Gentle Touch of Nature

Breezy whispers, gentle sway,
Nature's kiss at close of day.
Fluttering leaves like silly smiles,
Tickling toes along the aisles.

Fuzzy critters prance about,
Their playful games, a cheerful shout.
Rolling hills and fragrant air,
Laughter echoes everywhere.

Fields a-dance with colors bright,
Popping heads in sheer delight.
Sway with me, the day's almost done,
Together we'll laugh, it's all in fun!

Brightly Ripened Whispers

Whispers soft in golden glow,
Cheeky fruits, they steal the show.
Swaying high, the giggles bloom,
Tickled pink from nature's womb.

In the shade, the sun doth peek,
Silly dances, joy's mystique.
Round and round the laughter spins,
Crispy crunches, where joy begins.

Shimmering glances from the trees,
Chasing dreams on gentle breeze.
Brightly they shine, the world obeys,
In moments sweet, the spirit plays.

Golden Delights in Lazy Currents

In the sun's golden glow, where sunshine plays,
Laughing fruits dangle in humorous ways.
Swinging and swaying, they tease with delight,
Chasing away worries, they dance through the night.

Laughter erupts from the branches above,
As they giggle and wiggle, they share tales of love.
Jesters of orchards, their antics abound,
In this joyful circus, merriment's found.

Breezy Days and Sunshine Smiles

On breezy days, the laughter ignites,
With sunny smiles, we soar to new heights.
Fruits spinning round like a merry-go-round,
In nature's grand playground, pure joy is found.

A comical breeze tousles hats in the air,
As fruits giggle madly without a care.
With a twist and a turn, they swing all about,
In this whimsical world, there's never a doubt.

The Caress of Lush Green Flavors

In the garden of green, flavors collide,
With fruity delight, we take on the ride.
Jokes in the orchard, as flavors combine,
Tickling our senses, they're truly divine.

Each breeze carries joy on its playful wings,
While laughter erupts as the sunlight sings.
Green delights twirl in a jubilant race,
A cascade of colors, a whimsical space.

Fruits of Warmth and Whimsy

Under the sun, where laughter does bloom,
The fruits join the fun, dispelling all gloom.
In a whirlwind of joy, they prance and they slide,
Bringing warmth to the hearts, and smiles far and wide.

Bouncing around, they create quite a scene,
Adding charm to the day, like a frivolous dream.
With every sweet joke, the breeze gives a cheer,
The fruits of pure whimsy are finally here!

Swaying Sweet Symphony

In the sun they laugh and sway,
Golden skins in bright array.
Every twist a joyful dance,
Caught in nature's sweet romance.

Laughter echoes through the grove,
With each step, sweet stories rove.
Leaping lightly, all aglow,
A fruity rhythm, on we go!

Chasing shadows, dodging bees,
Giggling in the gentle breeze.
They drop a wink, then tumble down,
What a sight, oh what a clown!

In the orchard, sunny spree,
Nature's charm, a jubilee.
With every bounce, we feel the cheer,
Come join the fun, the laughter here!

Whispered Secrets of the Orchard

In the orchard, secrets flow,
From the trees, a gentle show.
Twisted tales of fruity fun,
Underneath the gleaming sun.

Ripe and yellow, smiles all around,
In this haven, joy is found.
Each fruit giggles as they sway,
Whispering tales of sunny play.

Silly antics on the vines,
Sharing dreams of wild designs.
Adventures leap, a grand parade,
In this sunlight, no charade!

Laughter dances on the breeze,
With every jig, our hearts appease.
In this grove, our spirits rise,
Endless joy beneath the skies!

The Sweetest of Breezes

A gentle breeze through green delight,
Swaying fruits, a comedic sight.
In the sun, they joke and tease,
With every gust, they laugh with ease.

Each little twist, a silly grin,
They throw a laugh as they begin.
Dancing softly, bright and bold,
A sweet escape, a joy to hold.

With every breeze, mischief swirls,
Crisp and yellow, nature twirls.
Jumping high, they tease the air,
In this moment, nothing can compare.

Such playful spirits in the sun,
With every sway, there's so much fun!
Their laughter fills the vibrant scene,
A whimsical, funny, fruit-filled dream!

Shadows Along the Path

Beneath the shade, a jolly crew,
Swaying low, bathed in dew.
Every shadow whispers loud,
Tales of fun that make us proud.

Footsteps dance on leafy trails,
With fruity laughter, a chorus swells.
In this paradise, we play,
Silly stories on display.

Jumps and hiccups make us roar,
Nature's chatter—who could ask for more?
With every curve, a chuckle flows,
Unruly spirits, how they pose!

As the sun begins to fade,
Joyful echoes serenade.
In this moment, life's a feast,
A funny end, a sweet release!

Elixirs of the Tropics

In the shade of palm trees, they sway,
Yellow smiles dance in the sun's play.
Giggling fruits in a grand parade,
Tickled by breezes, they've got it made.

They flirt with the whispers of the day,
Twirling and skipping, they find their way.
Chasing the shadows, they leap and roll,
With each little wiggle, they tickle the soul.

Under the skies, we gather 'round,
The laughter of fruit, such joy is found.
Beneath the warm sun, our worries cease,
With elixirs of fun, we sip on peace.

Join in the laughter, swing low and high,
Chasing the giggles, you can't deny.
In the tropics, let the shenanigans flow,
For we're all just bananas in this show!

Gentle Swing of Sweetness

Swinging softly, oh what a sight,
Golden treasures in the warm daylight.
Tickled by breezes, they swing with glee,
In a whirl of laughter, come join me!

They bounce and sway with a joyful grin,
Underneath the sun, let the fun begin.
With every twist, they tease and twirl,
In this glorious dance, the sweetness unfurls.

Listen close, hear the chuckles meet,
As they tumble and roll, oh what a treat!
In the gentle sway, sorrows take flight,
Under the sun's watch, everything feels right.

So grab a friend and come join the cheer,
With sweet little gigs and plenty of beer.
Caught in the moment, it's hard not to see,
Life's just a dance in this swing of glee!

Echoes of Lush Canopies

Echoes of laughter in the trees,
Golden orbs teasing in the breeze.
Swinging high up, with joy they call,
Welcoming all in the bright, tall sprawl.

Whispers of fun in the leafy shade,
A playful dance in the sun's cascade.
Tripping on roots and bouncing around,
Where the comedy of nature is found.

Swaying in rhythm with the skies,
Jubilant giggles, no need for disguise.
Under the emerald sky, we play,
Letting our worries fly far away.

So come along, join the joyful feast,
With giggles and swings, we're never ceased.
In vibrant canopies, we'll laugh and sing,
For every sweet moment's a precious thing!

Harvest Time Serenade

The sun is gleaming, it's harvest time,
Fruits are rolling in a happy rhyme.
Golden delights with a twist and spin,
Each little chuckle holds joy within.

Gather around for a comical cheer,
Lively fruits dancing, bringing good cheer.
Twirling and bouncing through laughter's embrace,
Every little moment, a smile on each face.

Chasing the shadows, they frolic and play,
With a wink and a chuckle, they steal the day.
Sweetness is bursting in every laugh,
A fruity parade on the sunlit path.

So raise a toast to the fun we find,
With giggles and sweetness, we leave behind.
In this harvest, we cherish the sound,
For in laughter's embrace, true joy is found!

In the Shadow of a Leafy Heaven

Suspended high in leafy grace,
Yellow smiles in a sunny place.
They wiggle and dance with silly glee,
As whispers scamper through the tree.

A monkey swings from branch to branch,
With clumsy moves, a goofy chance.
He steals a snack, a cheeky theft,
And leaves behind a fruit-shaped cleft.

The breeze is filled with giggles sweet,
As sunshine pours down like a treat.
The leaves all chime with laughter's tone,
Creating a stage that's all their own.

Each fruit a laugh, a silly jest,
In their green home, they smile the best.
With every sway, they tell a tale,
Of funny dances on a trail.

Rumbling Tides of Sunlit Cheer

Like boats afloat in golden light,
They rock with joy, a silly sight.
In the breeze they bounce and sway,
A fruity party on display.

The sunlight glimmers on their skin,
As laughter bubbles from within.
Each little wiggle, each soft quirk,
A dance of joy—a fruity perk!

The clouds below, they chuckle too,
At jolly antics in the view.
A tropical rhythm fills the air,
As mirthful echoes everywhere.

With every breeze, a giggle floats,
From leafy depths and scally coats.
In nature's party, joy won't cease,
As sunlit cheer becomes our peace.

Nature's Swing and Fragrant Echoes

In the grove where colors glow,
A happy sound begins to flow.
They swing and sway, a merry breeze,
Our laughter mingles with the trees.

Each juicy smile is full of fun,
Like rays of joy from a bright sun.
A jester's dance in leafy glee,
Where nature hums its melody.

The echo laughs, that fruity thrill,
As gentle breezes laugh until.
In the hum of life, we find our place,
With playful joy, a sweet embrace.

In every swing, a lightness found,
A fragrant cheer that wraps around.
The world around us starts to twirl,
In nature's grace, we spin and whirl.

A Cascade of Sunshine on the Wind

Oh, what a sight in fields so bright,
With yellow magic taking flight.
They flutter round on puffs of air,
Creating giggles everywhere.

Tiny critters join the spree,
As fruit escapes, wild and free.
Within the laughter, life takes shape,
A dance of joy, a fruity drape.

They bubble up, those sunny rays,
In nature's garden, bright displays.
Each playful toss, a joyous fling,
Embracing all that mirth can bring.

And as they sway on dreamy streams,
The laughter flows like lively dreams.
In every gust, a tender kiss,
A cascade of joy we wouldn't miss.

Driftwood Dreams of Tropical Bliss

On a sandy shore, I found a hat,
With a coconut drink and a friendly cat.
Waves are dancing, the sun is bright,
We're all sipping joy, what a funny sight!

Driftwood castles, we build with glee,
A fisherman's tale of a fish so free.
We giggle and laugh, the tides tickle toes,
As seagulls squawk at our whimsical woes.

Pineapple tunes strum by the bay,
Life's a cocktail, so let's play!
With flip-flops flapping, and ice cream melts,
Every moment's a treasure, pure joy felt!

The sunset blushes, wraps us in gold,
As stories shared turn to pure bold.
With driftwood dreams, we sail away,
Into a night full of playful sway!

The Sweetness of a Carefree Day

Woke up to find sunshine on my face,
Sipping lemonade at a snail's pace.
Laughter echoes, kids chase the breeze,
Chasing butterflies with giggles and ease.

Sunglasses perched with such flair,
A parade of ants scurries with care.
We dance on the lawn, feet feeling light,
Under a sky that sparkles so bright.

A hammock sways with dreams in tow,
While fireflies wink, putting on a show.
Chasing our shadows, we twirl and spin,
In the sweetness of life, where fun begins!

As twilight arrives, we'll gather around,
With tales and snacks, together we're bound.
For every moment spins a sweet tale,
In a carefree world where laughter prevails!

Tropical Whispers

A gentle breeze tells tales of cheer,
Tickling the trees, whispering near.
With giggles escaping like bubbles in air,
Every leaf sways, without a care.

Splashing in puddles under a light rain,
Nature's own wash, never brings pain.
We chuckle at storms that threaten our fun,
Because laughter is bright as the midday sun!

Sun-hats atop our heads held high,
In this funny dance, we never ask why.
Tropical fruits fling colors in play,
Every refreshing bite brings joy our way.

As night draws near, and stars blink awake,
Campfire stories bring warmth that won't shake.
With silly tales and giggles that roam,
In these whispers of laughter, we find our home!

Sunlit Curves

In the golden glow, we twirl and prance,
With floppy hats and a clumsy dance.
The grass is soft, like a comedy stage,
We tumble and roll like a youthful page.

Sunlit curves draw laughter from waves,
As we dive through splashes, like wild little braves.
With each silly flop and every grand slip,
We're heroes today on this sun-kissed trip.

Frozen treats melt, dripping sweet dreams,
As we laugh over sunburns, oh how it seems!
With sticky fingers and radiant grins,
In this canvas of joy, every moment begins.

When stars shiver softly in the dark,
We'll recall our antics, the wildest lark.
With sunlit curves and memories so vast,
In the heart of our laughter, forever we'll last!

The Rhythm of Ripeness

Swinging low with a laugh,
A slip here and there,
Fruits dance in the air,
Life's a joyous gaffe.

Flaunts of yellow delight,
With peels to the sky,
They tickle your eyes,
What a silly sight!

Sunshine wrapped on a bunch,
They giggle and pop,
Round and plump like a munch,
They never just stop.

Oh, what a grand spree,
On this sunny patch,
Making everyone catch,
A glimpse of pure glee!

Cascades of Sunshine

Golden bunches aflutter,
They bounce with pure cheer,
Skip along without fear,
As light as a nutter.

Branches full of good vibes,
They wiggle and sway,
In a silly ballet,
With nature's high jives.

A cascade of joy rolls,
With giggles and grins,
In this fruit-fathered spin,
Bouncing up and down poles.

Ripeness makes us all dance,
What a whimsy parade,
A twist of sweet charade,
Life takes a fun chance!

Joyful Sways and Tangles

Tangled in the green leaves,
They laugh with a jig,
Nicknamed the fun fig,
As the light deceives.

Wobbling to the beat,
They bounce in the air,
Whirling everywhere,
With small, silly feet.

Round they spin, full of cheer,
In a playful chase,
Finding the right place,
Without any fear.

A whimsical sight, indeed,
Twists of laughter glow,
In the sunshine's show,
Where joy takes the lead!

Chasing the Gentle Zephyr

Tossed by the soft breeze,
They tumble and twirl,
With a giggling swirl,
As light as a tease.

They flit like the bees,
In a chase of delight,
With petals so bright,
Filling hearts with ease.

Hilarious little drops,
In whirls of good cheer,
As they fly, disappear,
What a comedy, pops!

In this frolicsome ride,
They know how to play,
Dancing through the day,
With glee as their guide!

Dancing Golden Harvest

In fields so bright and sunny,
Golden treasures swing and sway,
They dance with laughter, oh so funny,
Beneath the skies of vibrant play.

The harvest's prance is pure delight,
With playful jigs, they jiggle free,
Their yellow coats in morning light,
Bring smiles to all who stop to see.

As breezes tease and giggles rise,
They leap and twirl without a care,
In every move, a sweet surprise,
A cheerful sight, a joyful flair.

So grab a bunch, enjoy the show,
Come join the fun, don't be shy,
For every twist, a laugh will grow,
In this golden dance, oh my!

Wind-Kissed Tropics

In the tropics, where the fun begins,
A playful breeze runs through the grove,
With laughter echoing, joy that spins,
A silly dance that no one can outgroove.

The rustling leaves share tales of cheer,
As golden gems take flight and glide,
They flip and flop with nary a fear,
In this wild waltz, they take great pride.

With every gust, the giggles flow,
A sunny spectacle, bright and bold,
In every swing, a vibrant show,
A comedic dance that never gets old.

Come join the jig, feel the delight,
As nature twirls in colors grand,
In wind-kissed hues, it feels so right,
Let laughter lead you, take a stand!

The Fruitful Serenade

In a symphony of sweet charm,
Golden orbs begin to play,
A fruity tune that warms like balm,
As nature hums, come dance away!

With every note, the zest unfolds,
A lively beat that makes you grin,
Each gentle sway of joy retold,
The fruity jam makes hearts spin.

They leap and sway in joyful sound,
A merry jig with every breeze,
As laughter rises, joy abound,
In this sweet tune, how hearts appease!

So grab your friends, let spirits soar,
Join in the fun, feel the serenade,
In every laugh, we all want more,
With golden dreams, let's dance unafraid!

Sweetness on a Swing

On swings of joy, they flip and fly,
With giggles soft, they sway with glee,
Golden treats against the sky,
A zany dance so wild and free.

As breezes push, they twist and turn,
In playful arcs, they take their flight,
With every giggle, hearts will churn,
In this sweet swing, all feels just right.

They bounce and jiggle in the sun,
Creating mirth that fills the air,
In playful chaos, laughs outrun,
A joyous scene beyond compare.

So jump on board, let's swing along,
With fruity friends, we'll laugh and sing,
In every spin, it feels like song,
Join in the fun, let laughter ring!

Playful Fruit Smiles

In a bowl, they bounce and play,
Laughter fills the sunny day.
Peels slip off, the joy's a tease,
Chasing shadows in the breeze.

They wear hats made of green and red,
Swinging high above your head.
With silly grins, they mock the cat,
A fruity party, just like that.

When the sun starts shining bright,
These little smiles take their flight.
Swaying gently, round and round,
With giggles echoing all around.

So grab a snack, don't hesitate,
Join the fun, oh don't be late!
These golden jests, so sweetly spun,
In every bite, you'll find the fun.

Graceful Arcs in the Wind

Twisting, turning, up so high,
Floating underneath the sky.
They form a dance, a silly twist,
In the breeze, you can't resist.

A fruit parade on summer's stage,
With laughter written on each page.
They sway like dancers, bold and free,
Serenading you and me.

Curves like rainbows in the air,
Teasing squirrels, without a care.
With every wiggle, every swing,
They bring a joy that makes hearts sing.

Whispering jokes in the softest breeze,
These fruits know how to please.
Let's join the laugh, let's make a rhyme,
In the dance of nature, it's always time.

Sun-Drenched Delights

Golden rays on vibrant skins,
Giggles burst from fruity grins.
A picnic spread, a playful quest,
These sunny treats are truly the best.

Rolling under bright blue skies,
With sunshine dancing in their eyes.
Sharing secrets with the breeze,
Making friends with buzzing bees.

Each delightful bite, a playful jest,
Nature's candy, passing the test.
With each squishy, sweet surprise,
These fruity delights are pure prize.

Join the fun, there's room for all,
Let's gather 'round and have a ball.
With laughter ringing, let's not wait,
For sun-soaked treats await our fate.

Shimmering Yellow Dreams

In a land where sunlight beams,
Live the sweetest, shining dreams.
Twisting up like acrobats,
With giggle fits and playful chats.

They shimmer bright, like stars at night,
A fruit parade, pure delight.
In every twist, a tale unfolds,
Of summer days and laughs untold.

Bouncing high on breezy springs,
Chasing after little things.
With every peel, a burst of glee,
In these dreams, we're wild and free.

So let us laugh, and let us play,
With shimmering joy, come what may!
For in this world of fruity fun,
Life's a dance, for everyone.

The Rhythm of Tropical Harvests

In the shade, they sway and dance,
Laughter echoes, a breezy chance,
Yellow smiles hanging on high,
Tickling the clouds in the sky.

With every gust, they swing and bob,
Creating a tropical, silly mob,
A raucous chorus, a lively cheer,
Naughty fruits bringing us near.

Beneath the sun, a playful tease,
Whirling about with such great ease,
Nature's pranks in leafy thickets,
Joyful moments in endless ticket.

From tree to tree, they take their flight,
A whimsical race, oh what a sight!
Bunches of joy, a fruity spree,
Life's sweetness flows, wild and free.

Wind-Swept Dreams of Sweet Delight

With laughter caught in the rustling leaves,
The sun beams down, and the air deceives,
A carnival of colors, oh so bright,
Nature's jester, what a delight!

Up in the air, a swaying parade,
Cheeky fellows in leafy shades,
They tango with breezes, like a dance,
Inviting all to join in the chance.

Whispers of joy in the blowing wind,
Tickling toes where the fun begins,
Frolicking fruits in hilarious rows,
Spreading grins as the laughter grows.

A gust of giggles in every sway,
Cheering the world to join in play,
With each twist and turn, they gleefully tease,
Creating a ruckus, a silly breeze!

A Journey Through Sunlit Groves

Adventurers roam in waved delight,
Chasing shadows, what a sight,
Silly bunches hang on high,
Winking at clouds as they sigh.

The sunlit path, a merry chase,
With giggles afloat in this warm embrace,
Bouncing along, no fuss, no frown,
Fruity jests in the leafy town.

Beneath the arches of emerald tones,
Playful whispers in teasing tones,
As the charmer wind joins the spree,
Fruits of laughter, wild and free.

With hats askew, dance like no care,
Life's simple joys hugging the air,
Every twist is a jest in disguise,
In these groves, where humor lies.

Harvesting Joy in Sun-Dappled Fields

Fields of gold in the sunny glow,
Frolicking fruits steal the show,
Laughter spills, a joyous song,
Where whimsy and sweetness belong.

With every gust, they flap and twist,
Mischievous joy that you can't resist,
A frosty treat under the sun,
This fruity harvest is so much fun!

Swaying bands in a crowded row,
Tickling giggles, making hearts glow,
From tree to tree, they sing and play,
Creating a party at the break of day.

Merriment blooms in endless sprays,
Brightening up the sun-kissed days,
In every corner, chuckles abound,
As sweet surprises cover the ground.

Lively Spins of Gold

In the orchard where laughter sways,
Fruits shine bright, joyful displays.
Chasing whims with a playful dance,
Nature's jesters, in a merry prance.

Twists and turns in a ripe parade,
Giddy moments, never to fade.
With a wink and a grin, they delight,
Golden treasures bask in the light.

Silly faces in the fruit-clad cheer,
Swinging and swaying, no hint of fear.
Echoes of giggles, a tropical song,
As the sweet scent of joy carries along.

The Road Less Tangy

Down the path where the peels do slip,
A fruity journey, a comical trip.
With a twist of fate and a playful jest,
Each step we take is a fun-filled quest.

Jokes in the air, they tickle the trees,
A chorus of giggles carried by the breeze.
Explorers of flavor, we wander and roam,
Finding pleasure in a flavor-filled dome.

The laughter erupts as we juggle and play,
Every splash of sunshine makes our day.
Oh, the road is zesty, with surprises in store,
With every bounce, we crave even more.

Hues of Sunshine Floating

In a world painted with laughter so bright,
Colors blend lovely in joyful sight.
With hues of sunshine, they shimmer and spin,
Creating a scene where the fun will begin.

Floating high like balloons in the sky,
Chasing away cares as they drift by.
A spectacle rich with each curve and croon,
The palette of joy dances with the moon.

Each burst of color, a giggle in the air,
Moments worth cherishing, beyond compare.
With splashes of cheerful, we whirl and glide,
In a world where laughter is our guide.

Golden Banners in the Air

With banners of gold that wave and sway,
Mischief abounds in the sun's warm play.
They flutter and dance with a jovial cheer,
A festival spirit, so bright and clear.

Flinging joy on a shimmering line,
Comedy grows under the sunshine divine.
Each twist and turn is a show of delight,
As laughter erupts in the soft summer light.

With a playful wink and a cheeky grin,
We toast to the moments that bring us the win.
Up in the air, let the party commence,
For life's sweet surprises make perfect sense.

Upside-Down Joy in Nature

In a world where fruits can dance,
One slipped on green, took a chance,
He jumped and twirled, oh what a sight,
While critters giggled in pure delight.

A wobbly stem, a twisty fate,
With laughter loud, they can't be late,
The sun shone bright as they swung high,
A fruity fest beneath the sky.

Echoes of the Orchard

In the orchard where flavors shout,
Fruits play hide and seek, no doubt,
A group of pals, they eat and share,
While sunbeams juggle in midair.

One cheeky grape threw a tart prank,
As oranges laughed from their high rank,
They tumbled down with bursts of cheer,
Creating joy, oh so sincere.

Sunkissed Surprises in the Canopy

Up above, a canopy bright,
Fruits in laughter, pure delight,
With every shimmer and every sway,
They play tricks as they dance and play.

A mango flipped, its friends all cheered,
As berries rapped, their beats revered,
In a playful whirl, they spun around,
While butterflies laughed and joy was found.

Juicy Dreams afloat

Drifting dreams in a fruity stream,
With every joke, they plot and scheme,
A pear slipped up and found its groove,
As laughter rang on every move.

The sky above, a swirling maze,
While fruity friends set hearts ablaze,
With juicy secrets, tales to weave,
In sunny laughter, they all believe.

Wind-Woven Wonders

A bunch of joy hangs from the trees,
Swinging and swaying with the breeze.
They dance on air, a jolly sight,
Making all the neighbors smile bright.

Their peels like laughter, bright and bold,
Whispers of stories yet untold.
In the garden, they do tease,
As they frolic with whimsical ease.

Chasing each other, they have a race,
With the fluttering leaves, they find their place.
Tickling the sky, what a grand display,
A fruity parade in the light of day.

So come and witness this merry spree,
Where joy is wrapped in yellow glee.
With giggles afloat and spirits high,
In this fun-filled fiesta, let laughter fly!

A Touch of Citrus Romance

In the orchard, laughter's found,
With citrus flirts that spin around.
A twist, a turn, oh so spry,
With each fruity wink, who can deny?

They flirt with bees and tease the sun,
A zesty tale of two, oh what fun!
Golden glimmers in the air,
Crafting romance with flair and care.

With every gust, they play their tune,
Swaying softly 'neath the moon.
Chasing shadows, making light,
These fruity lovers feel just right.

So let's toast to this fruit-filled delight,
With a wink and a laugh, it feels so bright.
In the realm of zest, let spirits soar,
Together we'll dance forevermore!

Harvest Moonlight

Under the moon, a harvest shines,
Silly smiles and fruity lines.
With a glow that beams from the trees,
Whispers of joy float on the breeze.

Gather 'round, my fruity friends,
Here's to laughter that never ends.
In the cool night, they break into song,
Celebrating where they belong.

With each chuckle, they sway and swing,
In the light of the moon, their hearts take wing.
Nighttime giggles painting the air,
As they whisper secrets without a care.

So join the fun under starry sights,
Where golden dreams dance through the nights.
With every sparkle, all sorrows cease,
In this harvest gleam, we find our peace.

Secrets in Sunlight

In the sun's warm hug, they spin and twirl,
Secrets hidden in a playful swirl.
With a chuckle and bounce, they bask in rays,
Creating laughter for all of our days.

Sunny smiles amongst the leaves,
Tickling whispers, fun deceives.
As the breezes carry their glee,
Joyful antics, wild and free.

With bright peels shining bold and bright,
They gather tales of pure delight.
In every swing, a story plays,
Their laughter echoes, a sunny praise.

So let's soak in this radiant cheer,
With fruity friends, our hearts sincere.
Embrace the warmth and sunny zest,
In this joyful place, we are truly blessed!

Leaves that Laugh

Green companions dance and twirl,
Tickled by a playful whirl.
Each ripple brings a chuckle bright,
Nature's giggles take to flight.

Beneath the sun, they share their glee,
Sprinkling joy like confetti.
Whispers of fun in every shade,
A leafy jester's grand parade.

Their silly antics, a sight to see,
Swishing, swooshing, wild and free.
In the canopy, laughter swells,
A comedy with leafy spells.

Underneath, we grin and cheer,
As they frolic, year after year.
In the breeze, their giggles spin,
A symphony of joy within.

Swaying in Golden Glory

In the meadow where they sway,
Golden wonders dance and play.
Tickled by the warm sunlight,
Dancing creatures, oh what a sight!

With every gust, they leap and dive,
Nature's laugh, they come alive.
Their yellow smiles so wide and bright,
Illuminate the day and night.

Bouncing lightly, they chase the breeze,
Giggling softly through the trees.
A comical ballet in the field,
Their funny tricks, they never yield.

Amidst the blooms, they spin around,
Bringing joy where they abound.
Chasing shadows, they swirl and bound,
In golden glory, laughter found.

The Playful Gust of Summer

Whirling winds with cheeks of fun,
Playful breezes on the run.
Chasing clouds and sunlit beams,
Tickling leaves like playful dreams.

Summer's laughter in the air,
Spreading joy, a light affair.
As the currents skip and glide,
Nature's giggle, our delight.

Waves of whimsy, skip and hop,
They twirl and twine and never stop.
In the warmth, their pranks unfold,
A merry tale that never gets old.

Watch them dance beneath the sky,
With each gust, they climb and fly.
A playful gust, so wild and free,
Breezy jesters in jubilee.

Circles of Delight

Round and round, they twirl with cheer,
Creating circles, oh so dear.
With every spin, they spread their joy,
Nature's laughter, a playful ploy.

In the garden, they form a ring,
Whispering secrets of the spring.
Their circular dance, a comic swirl,
As giggles bounce and laughter twirl.

Oh what fun, this merry sight,
As they dance in pure delight.
Together in a dizzy race,
Each loop's a chuckle, a friendly chase.

In circles bright, they spin away,
Spreading laughter, come what may.
Emblems of joy, forever free,
Circles of delight for you and me.

Nectar of the Tropics on the Breeze

Beneath the palm, they dance and sway,
A jolly fruit parade at play.
With laughter loud and smiles wide,
They bounce around, a yellow tide.

The monkeys giggle, swinging high,
As sunshine tickles from the sky.
With every twist, they catch a ride,
On nature's whim, their joy can't hide.

Through canopies, the whispers call,
Of flavors rich, they hold it all.
Oh, what a treat, this fruity feast,
A happy dance, a wild beast!

In silly hats, they strike a pose,
In tropical bliss, the fun just flows.
Each munch a giggle, each bite a cheer,
This tangle in glee, forever near.

Yellow Luxuries Amongst the Leaves

A golden smile amidst the green,
In nature's dress, a joyful scene.
They dangle low, with flair and style,
Creating laughter, mile by mile.

The squirrel joins in, with twitching feet,
A nutty dance to a fruity beat.
With every swing, they share their cheer,
The sweetest moments, drawing near.

Underneath the sky so blue,
Each bite a burst of sunny hue.
Giggles echo through the grove,
In this paradise, joy is rove.

With silly tunes, the wind does play,
A jazzy funk that steals the day.
And in this world of vibrant dreams,
The laughter flows like bubbling streams.

Petals of Sunlight and Soft Sighs

Amidst the shade, they softly glow,
With ticklish whispers, stealing the show.
A wobbly march on branches steep,
In twirling dances, secrets keep.

They giggle low, with playful glee,
A comedian's act from tree to tree.
In every rustle, silence breaks,
As nature chuckles, the joy awakes.

Through leafy lanes, their laughter flits,
Like gentle breezes that leave no quits.
Each sunny patch, a joyful find,
Inviting all, the playful kind.

With vibrant colors, bright and loud,
They twirl and laugh, all nature proud.
A festival of joy, a silly spree,
In nature's arms, we dance with glee.

Nature's Lullaby in Quiet Spaces

In the soft shade, a gentle sway,
With peals of laughter at the end of the day.
Their mellow tunes drift on the air,
A comedy act without a care.

As moonlight falls, they whisper sweet,
The sleepy sounds of a fruity beat.
Each sigh a chuckle from the night,
In tranquil spaces, pure delight.

The stars join in, a sparkling cheer,
While critters snicker, drawing near.
In dreams of yellow, night takes hold,
Of laughter shared, and joys retold.

So close your eyes, let worries flee,
As nature croons a melody.
A lullaby of charming grace,
In cozy corners, find your place.

Nature's Wistful Dance

In the orchard, laughter flows,
Fruits swinging in playful rows.
Leaves chuckle, swaying free,
Nature's breath, a jolly spree.

Breezes tease with gentle hands,
Amidst bright yellows, nature stands.
Sun above, with joy it beams,
Tickling trees, while nature dreams.

Celebrating the Bounty

Gather round, a fruity cheer,
Sweet delights, oh how they appear!
Laughter bubbles on fruity vines,
Joy ripens where sunshine shines.

Harvest time, a merry sight,
Nature's gifts catch the light.
Feste, oh oh, let's sing,
To the crops that make us swing!

Serenade of Sunlight and Yellow

Golden glimmers in the sun,
A frolic that has just begun.
Sway and twirl, no cares we hold,
In this dance, life's joys unfold.

Jovial ripples in the air,
Laughter twirls, free from despair.
Round and round, a merry tease,
With bright cheer, we find our ease.

Curvy Conversations with the Wind

Whispers dance upon the breeze,
Silly thoughts among the trees.
Curvy paths where giggles twine,
In nature's chat, all's divine.

Fluffy clouds join in the fun,
Chasing shadows; they all run.
Here, we find our joyful way,
With the wind, we laugh and play.

Nature's Melodic Curvature

In a land where fruits dance free,
The wind giggles, can you see?
A jester's hat upon a tree,
Nature's laugh, a symphony.

Swinging branches sway with glee,
Echoes of a bumblebee.
Chasing shadows, what a spree,
Whispers float, just let it be.

Lush Shadows and Sunbeams

Under the leaves, a playful scene,
Sunshine dapples, fresh and green.
A cheeky breeze, a rascal's sheen,
Nature's comedy, unforeseen.

Golden fruits in playful rows,
Tickling petals, playful prose.
Laughter bubbles where wind blows,
Life's a dance, as humor grows.

Breezy Hues of Yellow

Swaying in the sunny glair,
Joyful hues fill the warm air.
A giggle caught in breezy flair,
Round and bright, a fruity dare.

With each gust, the charm awakes,
Nature's pranks, it surely fakes.
Laughter pours like playful lakes,
In this world, delight it makes.

Laughter Amongst the Leaves

Rustling whispers, playful tease,
Beneath the branches, dancing leaves.
Chortles rise like bubbling breeze,
Mirthful moments, nature weaves.

Tickle the air with joy and fun,
Here, every shadow plays on run.
A fruity smile in morning sun,
Amongst the greenery, laughter's spun.

The Sweetness of Eden

In a garden of yellow, they sway and twirl,
Dancing gently, causing giggles to unfurl.
With a wink and a nudge, they steal the show,
Tickling our senses, bringing joy as they grow.

Chasing the sun on a warm summer's day,
A chorus of laughter, come join in the play.
Hanging in clusters, they brighten the air,
A whimsical feast, without a care!

The breeze whispers secrets, so sweet and sublime,
Each bite a reminder that nature's on time.
With a peal of delight, every munch is a cheer,
Life's a ripe circus, come grab a front seat here.

So peel back your worries, let giggles unfold,
In the sweetest of moments, let stories be told.
A fruity adventure, wildly absurd,
In a world made of laughter, let joy be the word.

Playful Spirits in the Field

In the midst of tall grass, they leap and they play,
Bouncing chums, smiling bright, in a golden ballet.
Swirling like catchers of dreams in the light,
Their giggles resound, a whimsical sight.

With mischief a-plenty, they bounce round the bend,
A chorus of chuckles, as if time won't end.
They giggle with glee, each tumble a score,
Their sunny disposition, who could ask for more?

In the playful air, mischief starts to rise,
With each twist and turn, their joy multiplies.
With every soft landing, a comedic flair,
Nature's own jesters, spreading laughter everywhere.

So come join the fun, leave your worries behind,
Embrace the delight, let your heart be unconfined.
For in this lush moment, let worries be lost,
As laughter becomes a friendship embossed.

Sunshine's Tangy Embrace

Sunshine is smiling with a tangy surprise,
Under the canopy, a feast for our eyes.
With a bounce on the branches, the fun's on parade,
Each chuckle a spark in this tropical glade.

Light as a feather, they sway without care,
A giggling melody floats sweet through the air.
The aroma of laughter, so fresh and so bright,
Bringing joy to each heart, a shared spirit light.

Tiny feet running, in sun-kissed delight,
As rays play with shadows, hearts feeling light.
With a taste of the sun, a whimsical jest,
In this orchard of laughter, let's savor the zest.

So let's make a toast to this sun-drenched affair,
Bring on the laughter, let joy raise a cheer.
In a world full of wonder, let's dance and embrace,
For moments of giggles, we hold them with grace.

Bronze Beauty in Flight

Oh, the shiny allure of a coppery hue,
Swinging through the air, with a charming debut.
With laughter on wings, they soar high and free,
A comical dance, come laugh along with me!

Wobbling with flair, they brave every gust,
Aerial acrobats, in sweetness we trust.
Each twist tells a story, each flip adds a wink,
In the sky of our dreams, we all share a link.

So keen to take flight on this whimsical quest,
Where mirth fills the skies, and hearts feel their best.
With joy catching wind, oh what a delight,
The bronze beauties laugh, from morning till night.

With every fun tumble, they steal the show,
Life is a journey where laughter can grow.
Embrace every moment, let happiness flow,
As we frolic together, in a dazzling glow.

Orchard Breezes and Tropical Dreams

In orchards bright where laughter sings,
Fruits wink and dance on playful swings.
A monkey dons a yellow hat,
And rides a bike—imagine that!

Clouds drift by, soft as a sigh,
While critters toss bananas high.
In this land of smiles and cheer,
The jester's song, we love to hear.

With every gust, the joy takes flight,
A tickle here, a giggle bright.
The sun peeks through the leafy greens,
As silly visions fill our dreams.

So come, let's frolic, dash, and play,
In orchards where the funny sway.
With breeze so sweet, the world's aglow,
Let's treasure every laugh we sow.

Sun-Kissed Curves in the Canopy

In the leafy realm, where shadows tease,
Sun-kissed curves dance among the trees.
A squirrel spins a playful tale,
As fruits swing gently, turning pale.

With chuckles loud and jests so bright,
The canopy's giggles send pure delight.
Laughter drips like honey gold,
In every breeze, a story told.

Rolling fruits, a merry parade,
Chasing sunbeams, never afraid.
Twisting together, we laugh and cheer,
In this vibrant world, joy's always near.

A playful wind, we take the chance,
To dance around in nature's dance.
With cheeky grins and hearts so free,
We celebrate this canopy glee.

Golden Spheres on a Gentle Wind

Golden spheres on gentle flight,
Riding high, a comical sight.
They tumble down with bouncy flair,
And we all join their wild, sweet care.

A gust of wind, oh what a ride!
They circle round, the fruits don't hide.
Laughter echoes, bright and wide,
As trouble's swept away with pride.

The balmy breeze, like tickled feet,
Brings whispers soft that can't be beat.
Rolling joy, as nature schemes,
A world adorned with vivid dreams.

So gather 'round, let's share the fun,
With golden orbs that spin and run.
In every laugh, we find our place,
In the joyful dance of nature's grace.

Lush Canopies and Jeweled Plains

In lush canopies where colors burst,
The world's a stage, we quench our thirst.
Fruits sparkle like jewels in the sun,
Ready for laughter, for playful fun.

Beneath the leaves, we sneak and slide,
Mischief waits in every stride.
The ground is soft, the air is light,
Our giggles chase the fading light.

Through jeweled plains, we run and dart,
With every twist, a brand new start.
We toss a fruit, it bounces back,
With silly cheers, we all must act.

So let's embrace this happy scene,
In nature's lap, oh how serene!
With laughter loud and spirits free,
In lush delight, we simply be.

Joyful Tresses in Tropical Breezes

In a grove where laughter thrives,
Swinging leaves do jive and dive,
With silly hats and sunshine's glee,
Nature's haircuts dance with spree.

Golden curls in playful sway,
Giggling branches lead the play,
Windy whispers tickle trees,
Joyful tresses, oh what tease!

Bouncing fruits in sunlit air,
Twirl and spin without a care,
Wobbly branches grin and twist,
In this land, joy can't be missed.

Swaying skirts of nature's dress,
Floppy hats, a lively mess,
Laughter swirls in every hue,
A fitting scene for me and you.

A Dance with the Swarm

In the garden, creatures swarm,
Under light, a lively charm,
Ladies twirl with flailing arms,
Buzzing friends bring all the charms.

Bouncing dogs in wild delight,
Wagging tails in morning light,
Silly antics all around,
Nature's giggles do abound.

Merriment with each loud cheer,
Chirping news in air, so clear,
Leaping frogs and wiggly dreams,
All unite in funny schemes.

Flutter by, you painted glee,
Join the striped brigade, you see,
One big dance on grassy floor,
Rhythms echo evermore.

Vibrant Colors upon the Wind

Colors splash as kites take flight,
Chasing rainbows, what a sight,
Up they soar, like dreams unfurled,
Whispering secrets of the world.

Bubbles rise to meet the sky,
Floating high, saying goodbye,
With giggles stirred in every hue,
Nature paints with every view.

Swaying blooms in jazzy tunes,
Under bright and merry moons,
Laughter threads through petals small,
A vibrant symphony for all.

Dancing leaves, a playful bind,
Spinning stories, sweet and kind,
Every shade a whispered tease,
Nature's laughter in the breeze.

Whirling Rays of Delight

Sunshine flickers with a grin,
Chasing shadows on a whim,
Footsteps dance upon the grass,
As sunlight beams with carefree sass.

Twinkling eyes in playful chase,
Each ray's a giggle, full of grace,
Splashing joy in every beam,
A sunlit, laughter-filled dream.

Wobbling daisies nod their heads,
As playful sunlight gently spreads,
Crazy hats take to the air,
In this fun, there's much to share.

Mirthful spins, a twinkling show,
Whirling rays of brightened glow,
Joyful hearts and cheeky plays,
Dance around on sunny days.

Grove of Golden Whispers

In a grove where laughter plays,
Trees jest in playful ways.
Leaves flutter like silly fans,
Fruit hangs in tempting clans.

Squirrels dance on branches high,
Plotting mischief, oh my, my!
A tickle of wind, oh what a tease,
Nature chuckles with such ease.

Breezes swirl with giggling cheer,
Even the shadows seem to leer.
Golden orbs sway side to side,
In this plot where jokes abide.

Under skies of endless blue,
Every moment brings the woo-hoo!
Joyous whispers all around,
In this playful, quirky ground.

Twisted Laughter Beneath the Sun

Underneath the shining orb,
Wacky antics start to absorb.
Chasing shadows on the floor,
Life's a joke that asks for more.

Funny faces in the grove,
Playful tales that all behove.
Side-splitting giggles fill the air,
Every critter stops to stare.

Juggling fruits, oh what a sight,
Laughter echoes, pure delight.
Nature's charm leads us astray,
In this silly, bright ballet.

Beneath the sun, where we all trot,
Ticklish moments connect the lot.
A playful breeze brings wild flair,
In this dance, we have no care.

Carousel of Flavor in the Air

Whirling whimsies spin around,
A carousel of joy is found.
Frolicking like kids at play,
Flavor bursts on a sunny day.

From branch to branch, it swings with glee,
Intriguing bites for all to see.
As each roundabout takes its spin,
Giggling flavors draw us in.

The fruit parade, oh what a sight,
Caught up in this amusing flight.
With each rotation, smiles grow wide,
In this merry, zesty ride.

Laughing clouds play peekaboo,
With every taste, find something new.
Round and round, we won't despair,
On this carousel, let's all share.

Whirling Grooves of Nature's Joy

In the groove of nature's jest,
Life spins on with so much zest.
Swaying to the rhythm fair,
Every being finds its dare.

Ticklish breezes start the show,
Brighten up this playful glow.
Dancing leaves in wild delight,
Whispers travel, take flight.

The silly critters bounce and prance,
In this magical, vibrant dance.
Each moment sparks a hearty laugh,
It's a joyful, lively craft.

Underneath the open sky,
Laughing echoes soar up high.
We join in this revelry,
In whirling grooves, oh let it be!